A Tale of Two Cities
In Plain and Simple English

Charles Dickens

*Includes Study Guide, Historical Context,
Biography and Character Index*

BookCaps™ Study Guides
www.bookcaps.com

© 2012. All Rights Reserved.

Table of Contents

Study Guide

Historical Context

Charles Dickens was born in England in the year 1812. His family was poor, and his childhood troubled. At the age of twelve, he was forced to work in a factory, and these experiences highly influenced his early writing, coming through in novels such as Oliver Twist. By the 1850's, Dickens was the most popular and successful author in England. However, not everything was going well, despite his success. His twenty-three year marriage was ending, and because of his fame, there were many secrets in his life.

It was around this time that Dickens began acting in a play called The Frozen Madness. He played a man who competed with another man for a woman's affection, eventually dying so that the woman could remain happy with her true love. During the course of the play, he also fell in love with a young actress. The play and the affair affected Dickens' deeply, and he decided to write a novel revolving around the same themes of love, cruelty, and sacrifice.

He decided to make the setting for his new novel the bloody and terrifying French Revolution. There were several reasons for his choice. First, Dickens was primarily a writer of social criticisms. During the late 1850's, there was a serious worry that an English revolution would follow closely on the heels of the French Revolution.

The 18th century in England saw the beginning of the Industrial revolution, which created a distinct class separation. As England began to see more factories and mass production, it became easier and easier for the few on top to oppress the lower class. Soon, there was a class of Bourgeois, immensely wealthy nobility, and the poor commons. The rich had almost unlimited power. They hiked taxes, lowered wages, and forced those in factories to work long hours in dangerous conditions.

It is this form of oppression that permeates Dickens' early novels. His main characters were normally poor, and the main conflict is to find a way out of their impoverished and starving state. As Dickens evolved as a writer, however, he felt the need to write a different type of novel. He thought a fictional, yet accurate, account of the French Revolution would show the people of England the dangers of oppression on a larger scale.

A Tale of Two Cities was published in 1859 by Dickens' own magazine All the Year Round. Like his other novels, it was serialized weekly and later compiled into a complete novel. Although it received mixed reviews at the time, today it is considered Dickens' most widely read novel. An English revolution never occurred, in part because many people, such as Dickens, were adamant about warning the public about the dangers of oppression and violence.

Plot Summary

A Tale of Two Cities opens in the year 1775. At this point in history, both France and England are experiencing acute social unrest due to an unfair and oppressive class system. The rich are insanely rich, and the poor are starving.

The first scene follows the Dover mail as it is traveling from London. During the journey, a messenger named Jerry Cruncher delivers a letter to Jarvis Lorry, a banker at Tellson's Bank. Lorry sends a response which baffles everyone: Recalled to Life. In the next town, Lorry meets Lucie, a beautiful young woman, and her governess Miss Pross. Lorry tells Lucie that her father, Doctor Alexandre Manette, previously thought dead, is actually alive in France. He was unfairly imprisoned, and later released. Lorry wants Lucie to help him get Manette back to England.

In France, Lorry and Lucie meet up with Ernest Defarge, the owner of a wine-shop in Saint Antoine, a town near Paris. Defarge takes them to a room where Manette sits in the dark, making shoes. He does not realize he has been released, and the eighteen year imprisonment affected his mind. Lucie laments over his condition, and they take him to England to recover.

The year is now 1780, and the scene opens in England. Jerry Cruncher is sent by Tellson's bank with a message for Lorry, who is serving as a witness on a court case. The person being accused is Charles Darnay, and the crime is treason for acting as a spy for France. Lucie and Manette are present, having met Darnay on their trip back from England and being forced to witness against him.

An up-and-coming lawyer named Stryver serves as Darnay's defense but does not have any success in swaying the jury until his assistant, Sydney Carton, steps up and reveals that he and Darnay are look alike; therefore, the evidence brought against him is merely circumstantial. After Darnay is let go, Carton, drunk, takes him to dinner. He gets upset at Darnay, but only because Darnay reminds Carton of the opportunities he lost due to his degenerate lifestyle.

The location shifts from England to France and follows the Marquis Evremond as he is going to a ball. His carriage, going too fast in the narrow streets, runs over a young child. The Monseigneur coldly throws a gold coin at the father in compensation for his lost property.

That night at the Evremond estate, the Marquis waits for his nephew, Charles Darnay, to arrive from England. Over dinner, Charles relinquishes his inheritance and his name, saying the family wealth was built on the suffering of others. That night, the Marquis Evremond is assassinated in his sleep, and a note is left from "Jacques", the name taken up by the French revolutionaries.

A year after the assassination, Charles Darnay, back in England, is in love with Lucie Manette. He asks her father for permission to pursue her. Stryver asks Lucie's hand in marriage and is turned down. Sydney Carton also is in love with Lucie, but realizes that he is not good enough for her. He opens his heart to her, telling her that he would do anything, even die, to ensure her happiness.

Meanwhile, Jerry Cruncher attends the funeral of Roger Cly, and English spy. In addition to running messages for Tellson's bank, Jerry is a Resurrection Man, or a grave-robber.

Charles Darnay ends up marrying Lucie. On the morning of their wedding, he reveals to Doctor Manette his true name, Evremond. When the couple is gone on their honey-moon, the Doctor relapses into his prison-state and makes shoes for nine days. On the tenth day, he recovers. When Charles and Lucie are back from their honeymoon, Sydney Carton visits and request to be allowed into the house occasionally as a visitor. In the next few years, Charles and Lucie have a child and enjoy a peaceful life.

In France, however, revolution is beginning. Monsieur Defarge and his wife, Madame Defarge, are two of the main ring-leaders. In 1789, the revolutionaries storm the Bastille. Defarge visits the cell Doctor Manette was imprisoned in, looking for something. The steward of the town, Charles' servant Gabelle, is imprisoned by the mob.

Three years later, Gabelle writes to Charles, begging him to come and save him from the prison. Charles, believing it to be his duty, travels to France and is imprisoned as and emigrant. Because he is an aristocrat in the minds of the French people, he has to die for the sake of the revolution. Lucie and Doctor Manette travel to Paris to find him, and meet up with Lorry there. Manette uses his status as a former prisoner to keep Darnay safe, and Lucie goes to a street-corner every day where Charles can see her.

It is one year and three months before Darnay is brought to trial. He is let go, only to be re-arrested later that night by the Defarges. After his second imprisonment, Miss Pross runs into her brother, John Barsad, masquerading as a French spy. Sydney Carton appears and demands a favor from Barsad.

The next day, the second trial is held. Defarge produces a letter found in Manette's old cell, telling the story of how he was imprisoned. Manette, a young doctor, was called to treat two peasants, a brother and sister, who had been injured by two men of nobility. The patients both died, and the name of the family who committed the cruelties was Evremond. The Evremond brothers had Manette locked away to prevent him talking, and Manette condemned the family for their evils.

After the letter is read, the mob demands that Charles Darnay be put to death by the guillotine. Lucie faints and is taken home by Sydney Carton. The next day, the day of the execution, Carton is let into Charles' cell by Barsad, who is the gaoler. Charles and Carton switch clothes, and because they look so alike, Charles escapes the prison undetected. As soon as Charles is with the family, they rush to leave France.

Meanwhile, Madame Defarge visits the Manette household in order to gather evidence against Charles' family. Miss Pross stops her, and a gun goes off, killing Madame Defarge and deafening Miss Pross.

It is time for the execution. Sydney, holding the hand of a young seamstress falsely accused, goes to the guillotine in peace. He makes the ultimate sacrifice for Lucie, and, in doing so, redeems his own soul.

Themes

Duality

The famous first sentence of A Tale of Two Cities "it was the best of times, it was the worst of times" embodies the duality that carries the entire novel. Throughout every level, the novel juxtaposes sets of two. Two countries, England and France; two cities, London and Paris; two forces, love and hate; two men, Charles and Sydney. Even Doctor Manette has two personalities. This duality was made to warn the English of the dangers of revolution by looking to the French, for example. By comparing the countries, cities and themes, Dickens hints at how easy it would be for England to fall into the same bloody fate as France.

Resurrection

The theme of resurrection comes through every layer of A Tale of Two Cities. In the larger picture, the French Revolution itself is a form of purification and resurrection. The revolutionaries have to destroy the entire society in order to form a new one. In the first part of the novel, Doctor Manette is "Recalled to Life" when he is rescued by Lorry and Lucie. Darnay is thought to be dead after his execution, when in reality he was brought back to his family. The most significant character to express this theme, however, is Sydney Carton. Unlike the others, Carton brings about his own resurrection. By sacrificing himself for Lucie and Darnay, Carton purifies his soul and is resurrected from a drunken assistant to a gallant hero.

The Power of Love

The main forces present in A Tale of Two Cities are hate and love. Doctor Manette, Lucie Manette, Charles Darnay, Miss Pross, Sydney Carton and Lorry all stand, in one way or another, for the power of love. Doctor Manette is brought back to himself through Lucie's love. Lucie commands enormous power in the novel, not because she is physically strong, but because she is loving and kind. It is this kindness that inspires unlimited loyalty in characters such as Miss Pross and Sydney Carton.

The Power of Hate

The opposite of Lucie is undoubtedly Madame Defarge, who represents hate and vengeance on an unnatural level. Although the Madame is the cruelest character in the novel, Dickens seems to have a soft spot for her, making it clear that it was her horrific childhood and lifelong oppression that turned her into such a villain, not her nature. Throughout a Tale of Two Cities, Madame Defarge is a shadow in the background, waiting patiently for her revenge. She is eventually beaten by Miss Pross, showing that love can overcome hate, but at a price.

Class Separation and Oppression

The reason the French Revolution came about was as a result of social unrest. The top "1%" of the population, the aristocracy, held the majority of the wealth. They enjoyed lavish lifestyles while the commons worked for barely enough wages to live off of. The class separation became so extreme that the nobility didn't even think of the peasants as people, but rather as property. The same social unrest existed in England, and it was class oppression that Dickens spent his life writing about.

Justice

The reason the French Revolution turned into a bloody massacre was because of the need for justice. The revolutionaries didn't just want better wages and more food; they wanted the ones who oppressed them to pay for their wrongs. It is this sense of justice that, when combined with the need for revenge and the bloodlust of the mob, led to the insane cruelty seen. Towards the end of the novel, those being put into prison are no longer even aristocracy. Many are poor and innocent. The mob's need for justice was warped by the violence to become The Terror.

Sacrifice

In order to combat the revolutionaries' warped sense of justice, sacrifices had to be made on the part of the good characters in order to win. Charles Darnay was not killed by the mob, but Sydney Carton had to sacrifice himself instead. Madame Defarge is killed by Miss Pross, but Miss Pross loses her hearing permanently. There is also the theme of sacrifice before redemption. Only after sacrificing thousands upon thousands to the guillotine can France be reborn. Similarly, only by sacrificing his body can Sydney Carton save his soul.

Entrapment

Nearly every character in A Tale of Two Cities is trapped in some way, shape or form. In the very beginning of the novel, Doctor Manette is trapped in France. Charles Darnay is trapped by his real name, Evremond. Sydney Carton is trapped by his bad habits and inability to stop drinking. Madame Defarge is trapped by her need for revenge. The figurative entrapment becomes literal entrapment at the end of the novel, when Charles Darnay is put into prison.

Family

Although not as pervasive as other themes such as resurrection or sacrifice, the theme of family runs through A Tale of Two Cities from beginning to end. Lucie and Doctor Manette are the first to embody this theme, as Lucie rescues the Doctor from his mental instability. When Lucie marries Charles, Doctor Manette makes significant sacrifices in order to include him into the family, and eventually goes to extraordinary lengths to ensure his safety. While for the Manettes family inspires love and loyalty, for Madame Defarge, whose family was killed by the Evremond brothers, her ties instead inspire revenge instead of love.

History

While A Tale of Two Cities is a fictional account, Charles Dickens tried to make it as historically accurate as possible. He openly used Thomas Cayle's The History of the French Revolution to get the majority of his information, as Cayle's novel was considered the most accurate source at the time. Dickens uses real places, names and political figures to lend the novel credibility, inserting his fictional characters, such as the Manettes and the Defarge's, into the middle of the revolution.

Characters

Lucie Manette

A beautiful young woman who embodies the spirit of love and kindness. The daughter of Doctor Manette, Lucie rescues him from his prison and nurses him back to health. Later, she compassionately speaks at Charles Darnay's trial, urging the jury to be forgiving. Because of her resplendent beauty and kindness, both Charles and Sydney fall in love with Lucie. She also inspires the utmost loyalty from Doctor Manette, Mr. Lorry and Miss Pross.

Doctor Alexandre Manette

Lucie's father, thrown into prison as a young Doctor and held there for eighteen years. During his imprisonment, Doctor Manette loses his mind and spends all day making shoes in order to calm his nerves. He is revived by Lucie, yet during times of stress reverts back to his former state. He has no memory of these periods and wishes to be strong for Lucie's sake. In France, he uses his status as a former prisoner of the Bastille to keep Charles safe in prison. Ultimately, it is his letter written during prison while condemns Darnay, in which Manette reveals the crimes of the Evremond brothers against two peasants.

Charles Darnay (formerly Charles Evremond)

Charles Darnay is acquitted from his treasonous charges in England and goes to France to meet his uncle, the Marquis Evremond. While he is there, he tells his uncle that he wants no part in a system that causes widespread suffering, and he wishes to go to England to make something of himself. This he does, become a French tutor for students. He falls in love with Lucie and eventually marries her. When he receives the letter from Gabelle, his noble nature forces him to go to France.

Jarvis Lorry

An elderly banker at Tellson's bank. Mr. Lorry is, first and foremost, a business man. Rational and reliable, he is one of the more steady characters in the novel, and because of this becomes a strong ally in times of danger. He has had a strong love and loyalty for the Manette family since he was first assigned to their case, and he is the one who instigates the rescue of Doctor Manette from France. He is a perpetual bachelor, and his love and loyalty for the Manette family stems from his need for a family.

Mr. Stryver

An up-and-coming lawyer obsessed with power and status. Mr. Stryver is intelligent, yet shallow. He relies on his assistant, Sydney, to do all his work for him while he takes all the credit. Everything he does is for pursuit of status, including trying to marry Lucie Manette. While Charles and Sydney express genuine love for the girl, Stryver simply views her as the most beautiful woman in England and wants her as a trophy. During the revolution, he expresses sympathy for the Monseigneurs who take refuge in Tellson's, and opposing the revolution.

Sydney Carton

At the beginning of the novel, Sydney is a low-life with no motivation or ambition. He works for Stryver and stays drunk all the time, never daring to hope for anything good to happen in his life. Because of his extraordinary similarity to Charles Darnay, he becomes jealous and views Charles as a reflection of the man he never was because of his bad habits. Sydney is inspired by Lucie's permeating kindness and falls in love with her. He knows he is not worthy of her love, but makes himself known to her. In the end, he redeems himself and his name by sacrificing himself in place of Charles Darnay.

Jerry Cruncher

The odd man job worker at Tellson's bank, Jerry delivers messages and helps with general errand-running as well as acting as the occasional bodyguard. He sits outside the bank with his son, young Jerry, waiting for work. By night, however, Jerry is a Resurrection Man, or a grave-robber. He digs up dead bodies to sell to doctors and medical professionals. Because of this, Jerry is superstitious and beats his wife for praying to The Lord. At the end of the novel, he promises to become a respectable citizen and to work for the cemetery digging graves instead of robbing them.

Miss Pross

Lucie's governess, Miss Pross is an enormous woman with red hair. She assumes the role of protector from the very beginning of the novel, where the throws Lorry against the wall because she believes he is hurting her "ladybird". Although she is a comparatively minor character, she represents the same goodness and loyalty that Lucie has. It is for this reason that Dickens chose her to kill Madame Defarge. In order to protect Lucie and her family, Miss Pross is willing to fight Madame Defarge to the very end and ends up permanently deaf from the gunshot going off in her ear.

Ernest Defarge

Ernest Defarge owns the wine shop in Saint Antoine that becomes the center point for the revolution. He leads a group of revolutionaries, Jacques One, Two and Three and is highly involved in recruitment and planning. Although he wishes the revolution to come and is committed to its cause, he shows true remorse for the innocent who are killed. He begs his wife not to put Charles Darnay's name on her register because of his ties to the Doctor, and later urges her not to go after his innocent family. When Charles is captured, however, Defarge refuses to help him because he views Charles' capture and death as fate.

Therese Defarge

The wife of Ernest Defarge, and the younger sister of
the peasants who were killed by the Evremond
brothers. Saved as a child, she spent her life harboring
her anger and resentment at the nobility of France
until she became nothing more than a cruel shell of a
person. Unlike other members of the revolution,
Madame Defarge seems to retain her right state of
mind instead of devolving into mob-think, which
makes her all the more terrifying because of the
atrocities she commits. Because of her past, the death
of Charles Darnay and his entire family is central to
her revenge. She does not care that Lucie and her
daughter are innocent, and weren't even in France.
Ultimately, she causes her own demise when her gun
goes off in her face during the battle with Miss Pross.

The Marquis Evremond (Monseigneur)

The Marquis represents the evil of the aristocracy put into one ominous character. He is striking, and his face is a perfect mask. The epitome of refinement and manners, his behavior is contrasted by his extreme cruelty to peasants, whom he views as so beneath him as to not even be of notice. After his carriage, his and kills a peasant boy, he tries to buy his way out of it like the boy was property. That night, he is killed by the boy's father. As a young man, he was one of the two involved in the crimes against the peasants that resulted in Doctor Manette's imprisonment, thus bringing the violence in the novel full-circle when Darnay is sentenced to death for the Marquis' crimes.

Solomon Pross (John Barsad)

Solomon is Miss Pross' long-lost brother. She thinks the world of him, but Lorry knows him to be a thief and a liar. He originally worked as a spy for England and testified against Charles Darnay during his trial. Eventually, however, he moves to France and goes undercover. He reappears at the end of the novel when Sydney Carton threatens him to do a favor. Barsad is one of the gaolers at the prison, and can allow Sydney to see Charles before his execution.

Gabelle

The steward who works for the Evremond family and manages the small village that supports their homestead. Although he collects some taxes, he is not a member of the aristocracy. When the Evremond estate burns, the peasants turn on Gabelle because of his connection to the wealthy family and imprison him. Three years later, Gabelle writes to Charles begging for his life.

The Wood-Sawyer

A French revolutionary who talks to Lucie as she stands on the street every day where Charles can see her. Unknown to Lucie, the wood-sawyer is actually a spy for Madame Defarge and agrees to testify against her in the trials. The wood-sawyer is an average joe who delights in the violence and death of the revolution, comparing his saw to a guillotine and making crude remarks.

The Vengeance

A mysterious woman whose real name is unknown, The Vengeance follows Madame Defarge everywhere once the revolution starts. She beats on drums and outwardly displays her bloodthirsty, vengeful nature. Her outward actions are a reflection of the cruelty present inside Madame Defarge's cold and calm exterior.

Chapter Summaries

Book the First: Recalled the Life

I. The Period

The first chapter serves as a backdrop for the social and political states of England and France in the year 1775. Both countries are ruled by a King and Queen, both countries have problems with their justice systems, and both are unfair to the lower classes. They each have their own unique problems, however.

In England, the citizens have developed a preoccupation with the supernatural, spirituality, and ghosts. There is rampant criminal activity, but the justice system is not effective. The judges punish everyone equally, murders and petty thieves alike.

In France, they are printing too much money and suffering from inflation. The country is religious, but perhaps overly so. For even the smallest religious crime, cruel punishments are invented and carried out, foretelling the invention of the guillotine.

There are no characters, but rather references. The King and Queen of England are referred to as "large jawed and plain faced", while the King and Queen of France are referred to as "large jawed and fair faced". The common classes are represented by the Woodman and the Farmer, who are always working while the King and Queen look down on them.

II. The Mail

The scene opens on a Friday night in November on the Dover road. The Dover mail coach is traveling through the mud and mists on their route, with several passengers along. On one hill, the horses are having such a hard time getting up that the passengers must get out and walk alongside the coach. Everyone is wary of the others, because highway robberies are extremely common.

When they reach the top of the hill, they hear a horse galloping toward them. The guard threatens the man and horse not to come closer, and the man yells for a Mr. Jarvis Lorry. Lorry knows the man, his name is Jerry, and tells the guard to stand down. Jerry brings a note to Lorry, which reads "Wait at Dover for Mam'selle". Lorry gives his reply to Jerry: recalled to life. He then gets back in the coach and the Dover mail continues on its way. Jerry, taking a rest, puzzles over the meaning of the mysterious phrase.

III. The Night Shadows

The narrator, unnamed, muses over the mysterious nature of humans in relation to each other. The passengers in the coach all have their secrets, things that the others have no way of knowing.

Lorry half-sleeps half-dreams during the night. He is an employee of Tellson's Bank, and many of his scenarios take place there. However, the thing that most occupies his thoughts is his mission, which is to dig up someone who has been buried alive for eighteen years. Lorry imagines scenario after scenario changing everything from the dialogue to what the man looks like.

The night is over, and sunlight wakes Lorry from his dreams.

IV. The Preparation

The coach arrives in Dover and drops Mr. Lorry off at the Royal George Hotel. After a haircut and a change of clothes, Mr. Lorry goes to the breakfast room. His appearance up until this point being concealed by a large coat, he is revealed to be a businessman of about sixty, wearing a brown suit with attention to detail. Lorry asks the waitress to make accommodations for a young lady who is arriving later, who will ask for Jarvis Lorry or the man from Tellson's bank. He spends the day awaiting her arrival.

After dinner, he is summoned to her chambers. She is a young, pretty woman of seventeen, named Miss Manette. She tells Lorry she was summoned by the bank because they had information about her father, long dead. Lorry affirms this and gently begins his tale.

Mr. Lorry tells of a French gentleman, a doctor from Beauvais who married an English lady. At this point, Miss Manette realizes the story is about her father and urges him to continue. Lorry slowly reveals that the girl's father is not dead; rather, he has been imprisoned in Paris for eighteen years. Miss Manette was summoned to help facilitate his recovery.

Miss Manette is shocked, and grabs Mr. Lorry's arm tightly. When she won't let go or respond Mr. Lorry calls for help. An enormous woman with red hair comes in and throws Mr. Lorry into a wall, scolding him for scaring the girl and calling for smelling salts.

V. The Wine Shop

The setting shifts from England to Saint Antoine, a suburb of Paris. A cask of wine is dropped in the street, and everyone rushes to get a drink. The red wine stains everything, including the ground, as well as hands, feet, and mouths. The red wine is a warning of the bloodshed that will come during the revolution.

In this part of town, hunger is everywhere, and desperation. The shops offer scant amounts of food to those who can afford it, but it isn't enough. The wine shop owner is watching the commotion on the street. A big man, he exudes a sense of authority, getting on to the joker Gaspard for writing "blood" on the wall with the spilt wine.

Inside, his wife is knitting and lets him know through covert coughs that there are new customers present. The couple is Monsieur and Madame Defarge. Monsieur Defarge ignores the new customers (an elderly gentleman and a young lady), turning his attention to three men at the counter. He addresses them all as Jacques, and they leave. Only then does he turn to the elderly man.

After they speak quickly, Monsieur Defarge motions for Mr. Lorry and Miss Manette to follow him. They enter a run-down stairway and begin climbing. Monsieur Defarge's countenance has turned dangerous. At the top floor, the three men from the bar are there looking in a cell. Defarge tells Lorry and Miss Manette that he shows Monsieur Manette to those who can benefit from the sight. Miss Manette admits that she is afraid, but goes in the room anyway. Inside, a white-haired man is intently making shoes.

VI. The Shoemaker

Mr. Lorry and Monsieur Defarge begin speaking to Doctor Manette, gently trying to get him to tell them about himself and his occupation. The Doctor seems incapable of holding a real conversation, and continually goes back to his work whenever there is a lull. He is starved and weak, and is reluctant to let the light into his room.

When he sees Miss Manette, his daughter, he is perplexed and in awe. He looks at her golden hair and compares it to a few hairs he has kept tucked in his breast since the beginning of his imprisonment. Although he doesn't have enough cognitive power after his long imprisonment to realize Miss Manette is his daughter, he is nonetheless drawn to her presence. She, in turn, comforts him in an impassioned speech, and hints that his sufferings will be over soon.

While she stays with the Doctor, Lorry and Defarge make plans to travel to England. They don't know if the Monsieur Manette is fit for the journey, but it would be better than keeping the man in that dark cell. They go to retrieve the pair, and find the old man confused upon awakening. It becomes clear that he never remembers being released from prison and going to the house, but he follows his daughter as she leads him to the coach.

Book the Second: The Golden Thread

I. Five Years Later

It is now 1780, and the scene opens on Tellson's Bank. A lengthy description is given, painting the bank as a dark, dingy place with old employees and musty bank-notes. The bank is located next to the Temple Bar, where the heads of criminals are put up as warning. Tellson's has sent quite a few heads up there as well, as they turn in their employees who commit small or large crimes.

Jerry Cruncher is the odd-job-man for Tellson's. He sits outside the bank with his son, also named Jerry, and waits for someone to give him errands to run. He has an apartment in a squalid part of town, and continually gets on to his wife for praying against him, though she protests she is praying for them. His son is an exact replica of himself.

In the morning, Jerry and his son go to the bank, sitting outside on a wooden stool. Soon, someone requests a job for Mr. Cruncher. His son sits on the stool, waiting for him, and questions why his father's fingers always have rust on them.

II. A Sight

The bank employee tells Jerry Cruncher to go to Old Bailey's, where a treason case is being tried, and give a note to Jarvis Lorry. He is then to wait there until Mr. Lorry needs him but doesn't say what for.

Jerry walks to Old Bailey, where the court is held, and is let inside by a guard. He sends his note to Mr. Lorry, and stands near the back to watch the "entertainment". The young gentleman being tried is named Charles Darnay, and he is well-bred and composed. His sentence, if he is found guilty (and a guard assures Jerry he will be) is to be drawn and quartered. Because of this, the crowd eagerly watches the young man, as if eager for his death. Jerry does not understand much of what is being said, as it is legal terms, but he manages to figure out the Charles is being accused of giving information concerning England to the King of France.

Charles Darnay is collected until he notices a beautiful young woman, and a white haired old man sitting in the crowd. It is Monsieur and Miss Manette from the previous chapters. Jerry, though he does not know their names, finds out from the guard that they are witnesses against the prisoner. The young woman's pity for the prisoner touches many in the crowd, curbing their fascination with the bloody sentence.

III. A Disappointment

The trial begins, and Mr. Attorney-General begins by stating the evidence against Charles Darnay. Mr. Darnay was spotted going back and forth between London and Paris, and according to the Attorney General must be guilty of passing information. After the Attorney General is done, Mr. Solicitor-General takes the floor. He questions Mr. Darnay, painting him as an unscrupulous character. He then questions Mr. Darnay's servant, who reveals that he made numerous lists, which he then gave to French gentlemen.

Next on the witness stand is Mr. Lorry, who may have traveled with Charles Darnay on the post from London to Dover as a fellow passenger. Mr. Lorry, however, refuses to positively identify Charles because all the passengers were wrapped in cloaks. Mr. Solicitor-General then turns to Miss Manette, who reluctantly answers his questions. Miss Manette talked to Charles during her trip back to England from France. Mr. Darnay helped her take care of her father, who was still sick, and made remarks about George Washington. Miss Manette begs for compassion from the court on Charles' behalf. Doctor Manette also talked to Charles three and a half years ago but doesn't provide any discriminatory information.

The Solicitor-General has gone through all his witnesses, and the defense, Mr. Stryver, comes up. He brings forth a man named Mr. Carton, who looks just like Mr. Darnay, as evidence that some of the witnesses may not have actually seen Mr. Darnay, but someone else. He says Mr. Darnay traveled between England and France for family business only, and not with treasonous intent. The conversations he had with the "witnesses" were nothing more than polite conversation.

The jury goes out to make their final decision. Miss Manette is weakened by all the excitement, and profoundly worried for the young gentleman. When the jury has made their decision Mr. Lorry finally beckons to Jerry, gives him a slip of paper with the result, and tells him to take it back to Tellson's Bank. On his way out, Jerry reads the piece of paper which says the young man is acquitted.

IV. Congratulatory

After the court session is over, Lucie Manette, Doctor Manette, Mr. Stryver and Mr. Lorry are congratulating Charles Darnay on his pardon. Doctor Manette has changed since his imprisonment, and is now a respectable member of society. However, sometimes his former depression sinks down on him, but not particularly often.

After the congratulations have been offered, Lucie and Doctor Manette leave the gathering to head home. When only the men are left, another man steps out of the shadows. It is Sydney Carton, Mr. Darnay's look-alike who helped him during the trial. He has been drinking, and Mr. Lorry chides him for not being a man of business before leaving with Mr. Stryver.

Carton takes Darnay to a nearby tavern to have dinner, and continues drinking. He is acting oddly and asking Charles Darnay many peculiar questions. Charles, exhausted from the day's trial, thanks Darnay for his help before getting up to pay the tab. After Charles Darnay is gone, Carton gets up and begins talking to himself in the mirror. The conversation shows that Carton sees Darnay as a reflection of what he has lost and is jealous of his attentions from Lucie Manette. He goes to sleep on the dining table, his drink in his hand.

V. The Jackal

Mr. Stryver and Sydney Carton are old drinking buddies. They went to law school together and work together on cases now. At Old Baily's, Stryver is referred to as the lion and Carton the jackal because of their personalities and ambition, or, in Carton's case, lack thereof.

Sydney Carton is woken at 10 in the morning by the hotel staff and wanders to Stryver's rooms. They get to work, drinking all the while, and Carton sits on the sofa deep in thought while Stryver relaxes. After the cases are finished, Stryver begins talking about old times, and telling Carton to try harder at life instead of being indifferent to everything. While Carton is obviously smarter, he doesn't have the same ambition as Stryver, and so has always been in his shadow.

Stryver changes the subject to Lucie Manette at court yesterday, calling her an angel. Carton dismisses her, and her beauty, before heading home. Stryver wonders what Carton actually thinks of her, however. Carton goes to sleep alone, thinking of how his life would be different if he was a man of honor and ambition.

VI. Hundreds of People

Four months after the trial, Mr. Lorry has become
friends with Lucie and the Doctor. He spends his
Sundays with them, dining and talking. When he
arrives at their house, they are not in yet, and when he
goes upstairs he runs into Miss Pross, Lucie's red-
haired governess. Miss Pross complains that
"hundreds" of suitors are coming to call on Lucie, and
that none of them deserve her.

Mr. Lorry takes the opportunity to ask about Doctor
Manette if he has remembered any more details of his
imprisonment: who accused him, etc. Miss Pross tells
Lorry that those memories are better left suppressed.
Doctor Manette doesn't talk about those days, and
sometimes at night he paces as if he is in his old cell
again. With Lucie around, however, he is much
better.

They hear footsteps, and soon Lucie and the Doctor
come in. Charles Darnay joins them for dinner, and it
becomes obvious that Miss Pross doesn't like him.
Lorry is still waiting for the "hundreds of people" to
show up, but none do.

During dinner, Mr. Darnay tells a story about the Tower of London. When the workers were rebuilding parts of it, they came across a cell with the letters D.I.G. carved into the wall. They figured out they needed to dig, and found a remnant of paper someone had written a note on. After this story, Doctor Manette becomes shaken. He quickly recovers himself when the subject is changed, however.

Sydney Carton comes over during after-dinner drinks. A storm is coming, and the group sits watching the rain. They can hear the footsteps of people running along the road, trying to get home as fast as possible in the weather. Lucie remarks that she always imagined those footsteps to be the footsteps of people coming into their lives. Carton remarks that, if true, it would be a lot of people.

Mr. Lorry has Jerry escort him home, leaving the group staring out the window and listening to the multitude of footsteps.

VII. Monseigneur in Town

A great lord, Monseigneur, has come to visit Paris. He hosts a reception for himself while surrounded by the most lavish luxuries. He has four men to serve him chocolate and is more concerned with the night's entertainment than ruling France. At the Fancy Ball, everyone is always impeccably dressed. The higher-ups have no expertise in their professions, and the women leave their children at home with their servants because it is not fashionable to be a mother.

One person, Monsieur the Marquis, is angry that the Monseigneur did not greet him. He storms off, and orders his carriage to head to the Fancy Ball. Men and women run out of the way of the galloping carriage until finally a loud thump is heard and it comes to a stop. A man named Gaspard is despairing because his child has been killed by the Monsieur's horses. Monsieur the Marquis survey's the situation, and flicks a gold coin into the dirt as payment for the child. A man named Defarge comes forward to comfort Gaspard and is thrown a gold coin, as well.

The Marquis orders the coach to drive on, when the coin is thrown back into his carriage. Angrily, he looks out at the crowd to demand who did it, but none answer. A woman knitting calmly (Madame Defarge) tells the Marquis to drive on. After his carriage is gone, others drive by quickly in a colorful parade, also on their way to the Fancy Ball.

VIII. Monseigneur in the Country

Monsieur the Marquis is traveling to his country estate by carriage. As they get closer, they pass through the poor village that supports the estate. The peasants are dirty and skinny, and all look down when the Marquis looks at them. Monsieur the Marquis stops on man, a road-worker, who was looking at his carriage as it passed by. The man claims to have seen someone underneath the carriage, but the stranger is no longer there. The Marquis grows angry and orders the guard, Monsieur Gabelle, to be on the lookout.

Driving out of the village, he sees a woman praying by a graveyard. She comes to him, begging for a marker to go on her late husband's grave. She says that there are so many people dying of starvation; there is no time to make markers. He ignores her and drives on.

After arriving at his estate, he asks if Monsieur Charles from England has arrived. He has not.

IX. The Gorgon's Head

The Marquis goes into his vast estate, admiring the luxurious quarters and the supper set for two. Since his nephew has not arrived, he sits down to eat by himself. Twice, he is startled by something outside the window, but he can find nothing suspicious. Midway through the meal, his nephew arrives. It is Charles Darnay, arriving direct from London.

They engage in small talk, but when the servants leave the room it becomes apparent that the two don't get along. Charles Darnay wishes to renounce his inheritance in France because he believes the aristocracy to be built on the backs of slaves. Monsieur the Marquis tells Charles to accept his "natural destiny" of being an elite member of society. Charles tells the Marquis that he is going to live in England, and the Marquis mentions the Doctor and his daughter while smiling in a suspicious manner.

Everyone goes to bed, and in the morning the common folk gather by the fountain with weapons. Monsieur the Marquis was stabbed during the night and a note attached to the knife reads "Drive him fast to his tomb. This, from Jacques."

X. Two Promises

A year after the assassination of the Marquis, Charles Darnay has made a living for himself in England as a Tutor of the French language. He has done all he can to forget France, his past, and the assassination. He has also fallen deeply in love with Lucie Manette.

One day, Charles goes to visit the doctor at an hour he knows Lucie will not be there. He tells the Doctor of his love for Lucie, and of his intent to begin courting her if she wishes. Charles does not want to come between the special bond between Lucie and the Doctor, but wants to be part of their family.

The Doctor, though agitated, agrees that, if Lucie should show feelings for Charles, he will tell Lucie of Charles' love. As a show of trust, Charles Darnay begins to tell the Doctor of his true family name. The doctor stops him and asks Charles to tell him after Lucie and he are already married.

Later that night, when Lucie comes home, she hears her father working on his shoemaker's bench. She becomes abundantly worried and calms him down by talking to him, and walking the room with him.

XI. A Companion Picture

Sydney Carton and Mr. Stryver are working in Mr. Stryver's chambers as usual. When Sydney is done with work, Mr. Stryver announces that he intends to marry. Before he tells Sydney who the lady is, he reveals that he is ashamed of Sydney's behavior when they visit the Manette household together. He calls Sydney a "disagreeable fellow" and wonders why he cannot clean himself up for a woman.

Sydney, changing the topic of conversation, asks who the lady Stryver intends to marry is. Stryver tells him it is Lucie Manette. He views Lucie as a charming woman, and thinks she could not refuse his position and wealth. At this news, Sydney begins drinking even more heavily than before. He tells Stryver that he approves of the marriage, however. Stryver tells Sydney that he should marry as well, preferably a woman with a little bit of money, so he does not end up on the streets.

XII. The Fellow of Delicacy

Stryver, having made up his mind to propose to Lucie, begins heading to see the Manettes. On his way, he passes Tellson's Bank and decides to tell Lorry the good news. Inside, Stryver seems to dominate the cramped space of the bank and tells Lorry of his plans. When Lorry acts doubtful, however, Stryver becomes angry.

Mr. Lorry tactfully suggests that Stryver should not propose to Lucie without knowing for sure if she will accept. Lorry seems doubtful that she would, and offers to see the Manettes on behalf of Stryver in order to find out his odds.

Later that evening, Mr. Lorry calls on Stryver, telling him that if he chose to propose the Manettes would reject his offer. Because Stryver is too arrogant to accept the fact that Lucie wouldn't marry him, he dismisses the whole idea, blaming it on Lucie, and asks Mr. Lorry to forget it.

XIII. The Fellow of No Delicacy

Sydney Carton spends his days drinking and wandering around the Manette's neighborhood. After Stryver tells him he decided not to propose to Lucie Manette, Carton visits Lucie one day.

Upstairs, Lucie remarks that Sydney does not look well and thinks he is acting different. Sydney tells Lucie of his love for her, and how he wasted his life away through his degenerate lifestyle. He reveals that Lucie kindled in him hopes and dreams, but that it is too late to realize them.

Distraught, Lucie asks Sydney if there is anything she can do to ease his suffering and lead him to a better life. Sydney says only to keep the knowledge of the conversation secret and never mention it again, so that on his deathbed he will have at least one consolation. He tells Lucie that he would do anything for her, even give his life.

XIV. The Honest Tradesman

Jerry Cruncher and his son are sitting out on the street waiting for business. They see a funeral procession going by, with a mob surrounding it shouting "Spies!" Jerry finds out that Roger Cly, the servant who testified against Charles Darnay, is dead. The mob hijacks the funeral procession, turning it into a celebration. Once Roger Cly is buried, the mob decides to accost random people passing, accusing them of being spies, as well. They begin plundering public houses before a rumor that the Guards are coming breaks up the crowd.

On the way back home, Jerry stops to visit a surgeon, even though no one is sick. Back at the house, he berates his wife again for praying and being religious. He tells them he is going fishing that night and waits for them to go to bed. When they are in bed, Jerry grabs a crowbar, a rope, and a bag before leaving. Young Jerry, curious, follows his father outside. Two others join his father before they scale the iron fence of the graveyard. In horror, young Jerry watches as they dig up a coffin. He runs back home, frightened.

In the morning young Jerry wakes up to his father beating his mother for opposing his business. There is clay on his boots when he puts them on. Jerry and young Jerry leave in the morning as usual. On the way to the street, young Jerry asks what a Resurrection Man is. Jerry replies that it is someone who sells bodies to surgeons and medical students. Young Jerry declares his intention to be a Resurrection Man when he grows up, and Jerry is proud.

XV. Knitting

The scene opens in Monsieur Defarge's wine shop. The owner has been absent for a while, and Madame Defarge has run the shop in his place. There have been spies hanging about.

At noon one day, Defarge and a road-worker called "Jacques" come in. Three men previously drinking leave one by one. After they are all gone, Defarge takes the road worker up to the room where Doctor Manette previously sat making shoes. He introduces the three men who have come up as Jacques One, Two and Three. Defarge himself makes Jacques Four, and he refers to the worker as Jacques Five.

Jacques Five begins his story. He is the road-worker who saw a man hanging under the Marquis' carriage. The man, who is revealed later to be Gaspard, has been hiding from the authorities for the past year. Recently, he was caught and brought to the small town where Jacques Five lives. After being put in the tower, a gallows was built, and a few days later the man was hung. The body still hangs, creating a shadow "poisoning" the town.

After the story is over, Defarge tells Jacques Five to wait outside. The four men talk about Madame Defarge's death registry, a list of all those the revolutionaries intend to kill. She keeps this registry in her knitting.

Several days later, Monsieur and Madame Defarge take the country road-worker to see the court procession. The man, in awe of the wonders of the court, continually shouts "long live the king". Defarge hopes that, by showing the road-worker the extravagances of the court, one day he will turn on the nobles and join the revolution.

XVI. Still Knitting

Monsieur and Madame Defarge return to Saint
Antoine, and the road-worker back to his small
village. On the way into town, a Jacques in the police
force gives Defarge information that a new spy is in
town - John Barsad.

Back at the wine shop, both Monsieur and Madame
Defarge are tired from their long day of travel.
Monsieur Defarge is depressed that the revolution is
taking so long to get going, but Madame Defarge
likens the coming revolution to an earthquake. It
takes a long time to build, but it will come, and when
it does it will be devastating.

In the morning, the new spy comes by the wine-shop.
Madame Defarge puts a rose in her hat, signaling
everyone to get out. The spy tries to get information
out of the Madame, but cannot. She refuses to
sympathize with the state of affairs, or the hanging of
Gaspard.

When Monsieur Defarge comes in, the spy addresses him as Jacques. Defarge tells him his name is Ernest. The spy continues drinking and tells Defarge that Lucie Manette is going to marry Charles Darnay, the nephew of the late Marquis. Now that the Marquis is dead, Charles is now the current Marquis. This news upsets Defarge, because of his loyalty to the Manette family. After the spy is gone, Defarge begs his wife not to put Charles Darnay's name in the registry, but she knits it anyway, saying his destiny will either keep in out of France or bring him to the revolution.

XVII. One Night

The night before Lucie is to wed Charles Darnay, she sits outside with her father. Normally they would read or engage in some other activity, but tonight they simply watch the moon and enjoy each other's company.

Lucie is happy to be wed, and promises her father never to let Charles come between them. The Doctor, finally beginning to come to terms with his long imprisonment, tells Lucie of the fantasies his mind had formed of the child he never saw, but knew existed. It is the first time he has talked to Lucie of what happened in prison. None of those fantasies made him as happy as he is with Lucie now, and he wants to make sure that she does not waste her life taking care of him.

At dinner, Mr. Lorry and Miss Pross join, and the Doctor has a smashing time. Later that night, Lucie goes to check on her father and finds him sleeping soundly.

XVIII. Nine Days

It is now the morning of Lucie and Charles' wedding. The Doctor and Charles talk privately in one room, while Miss Pross and Mr. Lorry help Lucie get ready. Pross and Lorry jokingly talk of Mr. Lorry's perpetual bachelor status and promise Lucie that her father will be in good hands while she is on her honeymoon with Charles. The honeymoon is to last a fortnight, or two weeks, and then the Doctor will join the couple in Wales for the remainder of the trip.

Doctor Manette and Charles come in from the other room; the Doctor is deathly pale, but appears to be acting normally. Everyone goes to the church, where the couple is wed. Afterward, Lucie hugs her father goodbye and she and Charles leave for their honeymoon.

After the young couple is gone, the Doctor begins acting strangely. Mr. Lorry notes that he looks lost and confused. Lorry goes to take care of business at Tellson's, and when he returns the Doctor is upstairs making shoes. He will not talk to Lorry or Miss Pross, and appears not to know anything. Mr. Lorry takes some time off from Tellson's in order to watch over Doctor Manette. He tries talking to him, telling him of Lucie, and going on walks to snap him out of his troubled state. After nine days, however, Doctor Manette still isn't any better.

XIX. An Opinion

On the tenth morning, Mr. Lorry awakens to find Doctor Manette reading by the window instead of making shoes. When he comes down to breakfast, it becomes obvious that the Doctor believes that Lucie's wedding was yesterday, and has no memory of the time spent in relapse.

Mr. Lorry begins trying to talk to Doctor Manette about what happened, tactfully asking advice for a dear friend. The Doctor understands that the friend is himself, but it is easier for his mind to pretend that the whole ordeal happened to someone else. Mr. Lorry wants to know what causes these relapses, and if they can be prevented. The Doctor replies that the relapse was foreseen but that he thinks the worst is over.

Next, Mr. Lorry turns the subject to the shoemaking materials, pretending that his dear friend is a blacksmith and the materials his forge. The Doctor, previously calm, becomes anxious. Mr. Lorry suggests that it would be better to get rid of the materials, but Doctor Manette tells him that the idea of relapsing with them to calm his mind would be terrifying. He eventually agrees to let Lorry get rid of them, for Lucie's sake, but not while he is present.

The Doctor spends the next few days in good health, and, on the fourteenth day, goes to join his daughter in Wales. That night, Mr. Lorry and Miss Pross go to destroy the shoemaking kit. They chop up the wood, burn everything, and bury everything else. The scene is compared to a grisly murder.

XX. A Plea

When the young couple returns, Sydney Carton is
their first visitor. He asks to talk to Darnay alone, and
when they have gone aside sincerely asks for his
friendship. He apologizes for the drunken incidence
the night of the trial, and begs Darnay to forget it ever
occurred. Darnay accepts his apology and gives
Carton permission to visit the household often.

At dinner, Darnay remarks that Carton is reckless and
irresponsible. Lucie is troubled by this and tells him
so later that evening. She insists that Carton has a
good, albeit troubled, heart and asks Darnay to be
generous with Carton. Darnay, not realizing he had
occurred offense, agrees.

XXI. Echoing Footsteps

The next eight years pass peacefully for the Manettes.
Lucie gives birth to two children; a boy, who dies at a
remarkably young age, and a girl. Mr. Darnay's career
is still successful, and Doctor Manette feels closer to
Lucie than ever. Several times a year, Sydney Carton
visits. The children love him for some reason. Mr.
Stryver is more successful and married a rich widow
with three children.

Throughout the years, Lucie still listened to the echoes of the house and streets. Like before, she imagines them as reflections of life. When little Lucie is six years old, the echoes begin to sound abrasive instead of musical, a sign that the peace in England won't last much longer. As if to confirm this fear, Mr. Lorry comes over one night. It is mid-July 1789, and his bank has received a sudden influx of money and property from France. He feels uneasy about the situation.

In Saint Antoine, the citizens are arming themselves with any weapons they can find. They plan to attack the Bastille, and the Defarge's lead the charge. Once inside, Defarge demands a guard to show him One Hundred and Five North Tower. This is the phrase the Doctor uttered when he was making shoes. Inside the tower, they find his initials scribbled on the wall: A.M. Alexandre Manette. Defarge and crew begin searching the cell.

Down in the yard, seven prisoners have been released and seven guards' heads put on spikes. The only one left is the general. Madame Defarge holds him down with her foot and cuts off his head with a knife.

XXII. The Sea Still Rises

One week later, Defarge brings word that a wealthy official hated by the common people named Foulon has been found. Apparently he was famous for telling the poor to eat grass if they had no bread, and feared the revolutionaries enough to fake his own death. At the news that he is alive the town goes crazy, especially the women, who, instead of being gentle creatures, turn into a frenzied mob.

The mob goes to the hotel where Foulon is being kept hostage. They drag him through the streets while he begs for mercy and Madame Defarge regards him coolly, knife in hand, as a cat would a mouse. Foulon is hanged three times before the rope catches, and afterward is beheaded. The mob shoves grass in his mouth and hangs his head on a spike. They also kill and behead his son-in-law.

After it is dark, the villagers head home. There is not much food, and the bakery is chaos with everyone trying to get bread at the same time, but there is a general sense of satisfaction and hope.

XXIII. Fire Rises

In the small village by the Monseigneur's chateau, the road-worker is approached by a strange, shaggy man who looks as if he has been living in the wilderness. They address each other as Jacques, and the man asks how things have been, as well as directions to the chateau. The road-worker gives the directions, and lets the man sleep until nightfall.

When the road-worker goes back to the village, he tells everyone that something is going to happen. Everyone becomes restless and gathers in the center of town by the fountain.

Meanwhile, the strange man and his three companions have set fire to the chateau. The servants beg the local soldiers to try and save the valuable goods inside, but the soldiers won't do anything. The villagers light candles in their windows and become so excited that they decide to go after Monsieur Gabelle, the man in charge of taxes for the village. The Monsieur hides on his roof until the sun rises and the crowd disperses. It becomes clear that events such as these are happening all over the French countryside.

XXIV. Drawn to the Loadstone Rock

Three years have passed, and it is now August of 1792. The French Revolution has succeeded in overthrowing the Monseigneur as a class, and the aristocrats have fled to England. Tellson's Bank, being a portal between London and Paris, now acts as a haven for Monseigneurs, as well as an information hub.

One day, Mr. Lorry and Charles Darnay are talking in Tellson's bank. Mr. Lorry is about to embark on a trip to Paris to retrieve some pertinent documents. He is planning on taking Jerry with him. Stryver, up for another promotion, is sympathizing loudly with the Monseigneurs in the house.

A letter is put on Mr. Lorry's desk addressed to the Marquis St. Evremond. Charles notices it, because Evremond is his French name. Mr. Lorry asks for information regarding the gentleman's whereabouts, but no one knows where he is. The Monseigneurs begin shaming him as a coward for abandoning his post. Charles Darnay comes to his own defense, saying he knows the gentleman. Mr. Lorry gives the letter to Charles for him to deliver.

Once he is alone, Charles reads the letter. He is dismayed to find out it is from Monsieur Gabelle, the steward of his estate. Although he was given directions by Charles to help the people with anything they might need, he was nevertheless put in prison. Charles is wracked with guilt over his servant's predicament. He decides to go to Paris, not only to save Gabelle, but also in an effort to do good.

He takes a message back to Mr. Lorry before he departs to give to the prisoner. At home that night, Charles writes letters to Lucie and Doctor Manette, explaining his absence. He leaves the following day for Paris.

Book the Third: The Track of a Storm

I. In Secret

Charles encounters many difficulties on his journey to Paris. In every town, he is stopped as an emigrant and questioned. He is allowed to continue because of his letter from Gabelle, and the escorts forced to go along with him. Charles does not realize how tumultuous France has become until he enters the town of Beauvais, where the villagers there demand his death for no reason other than he is wearing nice clothing. His escort says there has been a decree passed banning all emigrants to death.

When they reach Paris it becomes apparent that Charles is being treated as a prisoner. Once inside, he is sentenced to the prison La Force "in secret". When Charles demands a reason for his imprisonment or a trial, he is told that he has no rights under the new law.

Defarge is the one who leads him to the prison. Charles entreats his help, but Defarge refuses. He seems sad that Charles came to France, because of his marriage to Lucie Manette, but cannot help him. Inside the prison, other aristocrats are already there. Charles sees these men and women as ghosts of their former selves. He is sent to a solitary cell, where he paces, imagining Doctor Manette making shoes during his imprisonment.

II. The Grindstone

Tellson's bank is located in a former nobleman's house and has been taken over by the patriots. While Mr. Lorry is sitting in his room trying not to think of the horrors he has seen in France, Lucie and Doctor Manette rush in. They beg his help in finding Charles. Doctor Manette's status as a former prisoner allowed them to get through the villages safely, and he believes it will help save Darnay.

Mr. Lorry asks where Charles is being held, and Lucie replies La Force. Lorry, alarmed, asks Lucie to step out of the room. When he and Doctor Manette are alone, he opens the window to reveal a grisly scene. The common people are gathered in the square, and two men are operating a gargantuan grindstone. It looks as if everyone is covered it blood, and Lorry explains that they are murdering the prisoners at La Force. Doctor Manette hurries outside and is carried off in a wave of people chanting to help the former prisoner find his kindred.

III. The Shadow

Mr. Lorry moves Lucie, Mrs. Pross, and little Lucie
to a nearby apartment, leaving Jerry to guard them.
He waits all day for word from Doctor Manette, and
finally Defarge arrives with a note. The Doctor writes
that he and Charles are safe, but cannot leave. He also
writes that Defarge needs to see Lucie. Mr. Lorry
takes Defarge toward Lucie's apartment, and Madame
Defarge follows. When Lorry asks why she must be
present, she replies that she needs to see the faces of
Lucie and her child in order to protect them.

Inside the apartment, they find Lucie weeping alone.
Defarge gives Lucie a note from Charles, urging her
to have courage. Lucie, thankful for the message,
grabs Madame Defarge's hands. However, Madame
Defarge responds coldly to Lucie's gesture, and Lucie
looks at her as if in terror. Madame Defarge pays no
attention to Miss Pross, but is particularly interested
in making sure the child is Charles' offspring. Lucie,
sensing danger ahead, begs Madame Defarge to be
merciful. The Madame, once again, responds with
coldness. After the Defarges are gone, their
metaphorical shadow hangs over Lucie and Mr.
Lorry.

IV. Calm in Storm

Doctor Manette doesn't return from the prison until the fourth day. During those four days, over 1,100 defenseless prisoners were killed by the mobs. These facts, however, are hidden from Lucie, and Doctor Manette confides in Mr. Lorry.

He tells Mr. Lorry that he tried to rescue Charles from the prison, and spoke to the La Force tribunal. The tribunal refused to let Charles go, but guaranteed that he would not be killed. The doctor stayed during the massacres to make sure the promise was kept, and because of his skill in helping the wounded is offered a position as head physician of the prisons. Mr. Lorry notices a change in Doctor Manette, who is no longer bound by his fears, but is motivated and strong.

All over France tribunals are being held. The King and Queen are beheaded, and the guillotine becomes a symbol of the revolution. Many replace the crosses around their necks with images of the guillotine, and they are found in every town. Anyone who is suspected is thrown in prison, regardless of whether or not they are guilty.

The time passes quickly, and Darnay has been in prison for one year and three months during which the revolution has only grown more and more bloody.

V. The Wood-Sawyer

Instead of falling into despair while her husband in imprisoned, Lucie keeps her little household running smoothly. Doctor Manette tells her that there is a spot where Darnay can occasionally see from a window at three o'clock. Lucie waits at that spot every day for two hours, hoping Charles can see her.

Near the spot where Lucie stands, a wood-sawyer works at his business. He is curious as well as crude, but says it isn't any of his business. Lucie, instead of ignoring the man, talks to him daily and gives him drinking money.

One day, the wood-sawyer is gone from his shop. It is the day of the festival, and while Lucie is waiting a group of people, including the wood-sawyer, goes by dancing a warped and violent dance called the Carmagnole. Lucie shields her eyes, and when she looks up her father is in front of her. The crowd is gone, and there is no one around. Charles is at the window, and it is safe for Lucie to blow him a kiss.

Afterwards, Madame Defarge walks by and coldly greets Doctor Manette. The Doctor tells Lucie that Charles is being summoned before the tribunal tomorrow, and that he must go make preparations with Mr. Lorry.

VI. Triumph

Charles Darnay is called into the tribunal. During his year in prison, he has seen countless others called out and then killed, so he is nervous. Once inside the room, he is surprised by the appearance of the judges. Everyone has taken on the rough dress of the Carmagnole except for Mr. Lorry and Doctor Manette. Monsieur and Madame Defarge sit in a corner, avoiding Darnay and looking only at the jury.

At first, the crowd shouts off with his head and the judge questions Darnay warily. He tries Darnay as an emigrant, one who left France because of revolution. Charles argues that he left, voluntarily giving up his title and rank, to move to England. The jury isn't convinced, however, until the well-loved Doctor Manette gives his testimony.

The judge and jury finally won over, Darnay is pronounced free. The crowd is exuberant and carries him home on their shoulders. Charles gets the feeling that the same energy in the crowd could have seen him guillotined instead of freed.

Back at the house, Charles embraces Lucie. They cry and pray together, and Lucie lays her head on her father's chest, as he once laid his head on hers when he was imprisoned.

VII. A Knock at the Door

The day after Charles' return, Lucie is still fearful for her husband, although she knows she should be relieved. Her father reprimands her for her weakness, and he himself is confident that Darnay is now safe.

Miss Pross and Jerry Cruncher are getting ready to go do some shopping. Miss Pross asks if there is any chance of returning to England, but Doctor Manette says it is still too dangerous to travel. They leave to run errands, and leave the family peaceful.

A few minutes later, there is a knock at the door. Four soldiers with guns enter and demand the re-imprisonment of Charles Darnay. Doctor Manette, shocked, demands to know who demands the imprisonment and why. Because of their respect for the doctor, a solder tells him that Monsieur and Madame Defarge ordered his arrest, as well as one other, whose identity is not revealed.

VIII. A Hand at Cards

While Miss Pross and Jerry Cruncher are running errands, they go into a wine shop. Miss Pross, seeing a man inside and recognizing him, screams. She tearfully greets her long-lost brother, Solomon, who is angry at her outburst. Solomon is working as a French spy, and she could blow his cover.

Outside, Miss Pross tries to get Solomon's affections. Jerry Cruncher knows he has seen the man before, but has trouble placing him. Sydney Carton appears behind Cruncher, identifying Solomon as Barsad, the police witness at Darnay's trial in England. Carton tells Barsad that he knows of his status as a spy, and threatens to reveal him as an Englishman unless he accompanies him to Tellson's. Carton takes Miss Pross' arm to escort her home where she can calm down, and she notices a strange sense of purpose in Carton she has never seen before.

Once the men are at Tellson's Carton tells Mr. Lorry that Darnay has been imprisoned again. He is shaken that even Doctor Manette's powerful influence could not prevent the arrest. He wants Barsad's help and threatens to turn him in as an English spy. Barsad denies the allegations, and Carton says he saw him conversing with Roger Cly, another English spy, just yesterday. Barsad pulls a slip of paper from his wallet proving Cly's death in defense to Carton's allegations. Jerry Cruncher, however, knows for a fact that Roger Cly's casket contained nothing but dirt and rocks.

Out of defenses, Barsad agrees to help Carton. Carton wants to know if Barsad has access to the prison. He does and goes into the next room to talk to Carton alone.

IX. The Game Made

Mr. Lorry is angry at Jerry for having an "unlawful occupation" outside of his work for Tellson's. Jerry defends himself, saying that many of the customers at Tellson's are doctors, and used his service. Mr. Lorry cannot condemn Jerry when the business is two-sided. He apologizes, however, and begs Mr. Lorry to let his son continue doing odd jobs for the bank. He himself vows to become a gravedigger instead of a grave-robber, to atone for what he has done. Mr. Lorry will forgive him if he repents with his actions.

Mr. Barsad and Carton emerge from the other room. All Carton could ensure was access to the prisoner once before his execution. Mr. Lorry, who had gotten his hopes up that Darnay might be saved, is crushed. He reflects on his long life and sorrows for Lucie and Manette. Carton sympathizes with him, telling Lorry that he is like a father to him.

They walk together to Lucie's house, but Carton does not go inside. Instead, he wanders the streets of Paris. He decides to go to the corner Lucie often stood at, to be nearer to her. The wood-sawyer is there, and talks about the sixty-three who were executed that day. Carton, feeling sick, leaves. He goes to a chemist, where he receives two substances the owner tells him not to mix. Still awake, he keeps wandering until the morning of the trial arrives.

When Carton gets to the trial, he sees Lucie for the first time since coming to Paris, and is reminded of how good she is. The trial begins, and the ones who condemn Darnay are Monsieur Defarge, Madame Defarge, and Alexandre Manette. Doctor Manette, outraged, demands that he is being set up. In response, Defarge comes forward with a letter found in Doctor Manette's old cell at the Bastille, in room one hundred and five north tower. Doctor Manette goes cold and sits down while Defarge begins to read.

X. The Substance of the Shadow

The letter was written in 1767 while Manette was in prison. He begins telling his story. In 1757, he is walking one night when two men, armed, ask him to get into a carriage. He is taken by the men, twin brothers, to a house where two people are dying. One is beautiful young woman in a feverish rage. Manette gives her medicine, and when she is calm goes to the other patient. It is a common-born young man who turns out to be the woman's sister.

The young man tells Manette that the two brothers wanted his sister for themselves. They killed her husband and father and raped her repeatedly. The brother hid his youngest sister before coming back with a sword for revenge. He was wounded during his duel and is dying fast.

The young woman lives for a week longer, before finally passing away. The twin brothers don't even treat her and her brother like human beings, but like animals. They threaten Doctor Manette to keep the incident a secret.

Back at home, Manette receives a kindly woman as a visitor. She is the wife of the Marquis St. Evremond, one of the twins. She wishes to atone for her husband's wrongs, and help the remaining peasant girl if she can be found. Little Charles is with her, and vows to right the wrongs of his family.

That night, Doctor Manette is taken away to the prison. After ten years of imprisonment, he denounces all of the Evremond family. After hearing the letter, the crowd goes wild with bloodlust, and Darnay is sentenced to death within twenty-four hours.

XI. Dusk

While the crowd leaves, Lucie remains composed for her husband's sake, although she is devastated inside. She begs the remaining gaoler, John Barsad, to allow her to embrace her husband one last time. They embrace, and give their farewells. Doctor Manette is upset at the letter, but Darnay assures him that he only holds the highest respect for him, now knowing what he overcame to accept Darnay into the family.

After Darnay is taken back to his cell, Lucie faints. Sydney Carton, who has been waiting the whole time, gently picks her up and takes her back to the apartment. When she is in bed, still unconscious, he kisses her and whispers "a life you love". Downstairs, Sydney talks with Lorry and Doctor Manette. He urges the Doctor to try and sway the judges one last time. After the Doctor is gone, Lorry laments that there is no hope, and Sydney agrees.

XII. Darkness

Out on the street, Sydney debates whether or not to
visit Defarge's wine shop. He decides to go, and
orders wine while listening in the Defarge's
conversation. The Defarge's remark on how similar
he looks to Evremond. Monsieur Defarge is pleading
for the killing of Darnay's family to stop, for the
Doctor's sake. Madame Defarge, however, expresses
a violent hatred toward the entire family, and vows
not to stop until they are all dead. She is the sister
who escaped in Doctor Manette's tale, and wants
revenge against all the Evremonds.

Sydney, after hearing this intelligence, goes to
Tellson's. They wait for Doctor Manette, and when he
comes back late that night he has reverted back into
his desolate state. He asks them where his shoemaking bench is and begins moaning. They calm him
as best they can, and Sydney finds the papers for him
and his family to leave France. He gives the papers to
Mr. Lorry, and tells him to make sure that the family
leaves at two o'clock tomorrow. He tells Lorry of the
danger Madame Defarge poses and says that to stay
in France will be certain death for them. Sydney also
gives Mr. Lorry his own papers as well, but won't say
why he wants Mr. Lorry to hold on to them.

The plans being made, Lorry and Sydney escort the Doctor back to the house where Lucie is waiting. Sydney does not go inside, but looks towards Lucie's window and bids Farewell.

XIII. Fifty-Two

In the prison, fifty-two people are condemned to die the next day. Many of them by this point in the revolution are not even aristocrats, but poor who were accused of various crimes. Darnay, alone in his cell, mentally prepares himself for death. He writes letters to Lucie, Doctor Manette, and Mr. Lorry.

The next morning, he counts the hours until his execution. Two hours before, he hears footsteps in the hallway and Carton enters his cell, let in by Barsad. Darnay notices that his face has an unusual brightness in it and wonders why. Carton gets Darnay to switch clothes with him, dictate a letter, and then drugs him with the substance he received from the chemist. Carton calls Barsad back and orders him to take the fainted Darnay, now disguised as Carton, to the carriage awaiting departure from the city.

Once alone, Carton waits peacefully. At two o'clock, all the fifty-two prisoners are called together. A young seamstress who knew Darnay at La Force, frightened, asks "Darnay" if she can hold his hand for courage. When she looks at his face, she realizes it is not actually Darnay. Carton tells her he is dying for Darnay, as well as his wife and child.

Outside the prison, Mr. Lorry is leading the party out of the city. They are stopped by the guards and their identities checked before being allowed to continue on their way. Once out of the city walls, they are afraid of being pursued.

XIV. The Knitting Done

Madame Defarge decides to go after Lucie and her family, including the Doctor. She thinks that, if she goes to Lucie's apartments she will find her grieving for her husband. Grief for a condemned is a crime that Madame Defarge wishes to use against her in trial. She doesn't trust her husband because of his weakness for the Doctor and decides to act quickly, leaving that afternoon.

Meanwhile, at the apartment, the carriage has departed. Miss Pross and Jerry Cruncher stay behind to give the coach the best possible chance of leaving France. They plan on traveling out and meeting the others on the road to England. Jerry goes to secure a coach, and Miss Pross begins getting ready for the journey. They agree to meet at the cathedral at three o'clock.

Inside the apartment, Miss Pross is getting ready when Madame Defarge appears. Startled, Miss Pross acts quickly, closing all the doors to prevent Madame Defarge seeing the hurried packing and standing in front of Lucie's door as if guarding it. Madame Defarge asks, in French, to see Lucie. Miss Pross replies in English that she will never let her through. Even though they speak in different languages, it is clear that they are enemies. Miss Pross is shown as a defender for the family, and her strength comes from love of Lucie. Madame Defarge, on the other hand, is filled with hate against the Evremonds.

The two women, both determined, face off against one another. After waiting a few minutes, Madame Defarge guesses that the family has escaped Paris. She lunges towards Miss Pross and they begin grappling. Miss Pross is bigger and stronger than Madame Defarge and puts her in a hold. Madame Defarge manages to pull out a gun, but Miss Pross instinctively hits her hand, causing the gun to go off in Madame Defarge's face.

Miss Pross, nervous, continues getting ready. She locks the doors, drops the key in the river, and meets Jerry at the cathedral as planned. She reveals to him that she can't hear anything, and indeed, is permanently deaf from the sound of the gun-shot.

XV. The Footsteps Die Out Forever

The fifty-two prisoners are carted towards the guillotine. The crowd, used to the procession, is still curious about Evremond and look for him among the prisoners. They see him holding the hand of a common girl, and talking to her gently.

The clock strikes three, and it is time for the execution to begin. Some of the women wonder where Madame Defarge is, but settle down to watch the executions. They methodically count each head that rolls. Carton is still holding the hand of the young seamstress. She hopes that the revolution will make it so that her younger sister won't starve. Carton comforts her, telling her that they are going to a place of peace. They kiss, and the girl goes to the guillotine tranquilly. She is number twenty-two. Carton goes next, number twenty-three, and later many of the spectators note that his face was utterly at peace when he died.

The narrator allows Carton to imagine the future, in which France escapes the bloody revolution to blossom once again. He imagines Lucie and Charles having a child, a boy, and naming the boy after him. Doctor Manette and Lorry live long, peaceful lives in England. By dying in place of Darnay, Sydney Carton redeems his own soul, purifying it and ensuring that his friends will always remember him as a noble man. This is what allows him to go to his final resting place in peace.

About BookCaps

We all need refreshers every now and then. Whether you are a student trying to cram for that big final, or someone just trying to understand a book more, BookCaps can help. We are a small, but growing company, and are adding titles every month.

Visit www.bookcaps.com to see more of our books, or contact us with any questions.

Made in the USA
Middletown, DE
12 January 2017